A Town of Champions

….A History of the Carmel Dads' Club

Compiled

By

Dan Chapman and Pam Shepherd Otten

Dedication

This book is dedicated to Dick Nyers, the beloved father of Carmel football. Coach Nyers's demands of a winning attitude and playing by the rules will always be a part of the lives of the boys fortunate to be members of his teams. His vision of winning led to the creation of the youth program destined to become the wildly successful Carmel Dads' Club.

Timeline of the

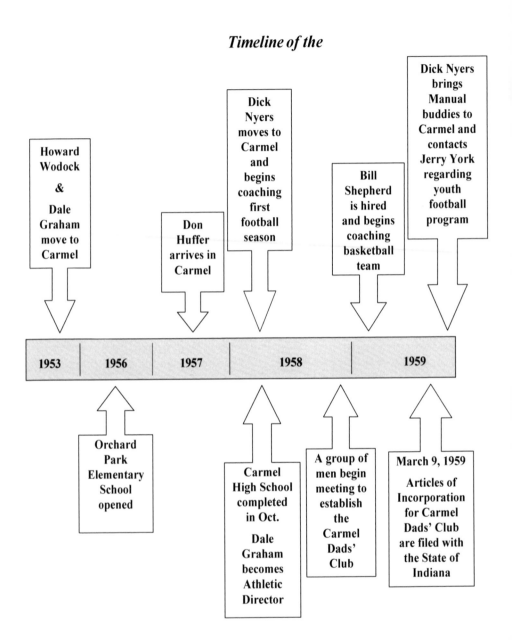

Howard Wodock & Dale Graham move to Carmel

Don Huffer arrives in Carmel

Dick Nyers moves to Carmel and begins coaching first football season

Bill Shepherd is hired and begins coaching basketball team

Dick Nyers brings Manual buddies to Carmel and contacts Jerry York regarding youth football program

| 1953 | 1956 | 1957 | 1958 | 1959 |

Orchard Park Elementary School opened

Carmel High School completed in Oct.

Dale Graham becomes Athletic Director

A group of men begin meeting to establish the Carmel Dads' Club

March 9, 1959

Articles of Incorporation for Carmel Dads' Club are filed with the State of Indiana

Carmel Dads' Club

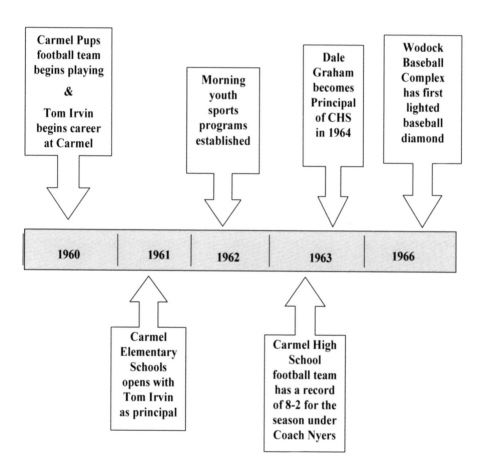

Carmel Pups football team begins playing

&

Tom Irvin begins career at Carmel

Morning youth sports programs established

Dale Graham becomes Principal of CHS in 1964

Wodock Baseball Complex has first lighted baseball diamond

| 1960 | 1961 | 1962 | 1963 | 1966 |

Carmel Elementary Schools opens with Tom Irvin as principal

Carmel High School football team has a record of 8-2 for the season under Coach Nyers

FOREWORD

By

Mike Howard

This book compiles the stories of a few ambitious pioneers who helped establish part of the foundation for the growth of Carmel in the late 1950's. During this time, Carmel was just a small dot on the Indiana state map. Interestingly, the dot for Home Place where I grew up was the same size as the dot for Carmel. Many of us, who were there during those early years of Carmel's development, can cite numerous reasons or list hundreds of individuals who have contributed to the growth and success which has made Carmel what it is 50 years later.

Whenever anyone defines quality of life in a community, opportunities for our children are always at or near the top of that list. The people of Carmel have always considered children's activities, primarily Carmel Dads' Club sports, as one of the community's invaluable assets. This book captures many of the stories of the dedicated individuals who laid the foundation for the excellence in youth sports programs in Carmel. I believe Carmel's ability to continue to excel in opportunities in the 1960's and 1970's has been a major factor in the growth and its overall success as a community.

I was fortunate enough to grow up in the middle of the stories presented in this book. My first baseball coach at age 9 in 1958, was Neil Schmeltekopf. I was terrible, but I never held it against Neil. In junior high and high school from 1962-1967, I umpired countless baseball games and refereed numerous basketball games for Carmel Dads' Club. My parents, Walt and May, managed the concession stand for the Dads' Club at the high school and Wodock Field for ten years beginning in 1962. They coordinated all volunteer concession workers and spent hundreds of hours setting up and tearing down after the events. The profits from selling candy, Cokes, and popcorn (mostly $.10 apiece), were divided between the High School Athletic Department and the Dads' Club. I was the first paid employee of the Dads' Club. My job was to cut the grass, line the bases, and clean the restrooms and concession stand at

Wodock Field for $35.00 a week. During those times, I met most of the people in this book and honestly took their efforts for granted. Forty years later, I realize how special these people were.

In consulting on this book, I have wondered what allowed Carmel to excel sooner and more successfully than other communities. I believe that Dick Nyers, who was my football coach in high school, touched upon the spark which led to this unrivaled success. I still consider his energy, desire, and dedication to succeeding as being a very important part of my personal development. In an interview for this book in the fall of 2012, Dan, Pam, and I visited with Coach Nyers. We discussed many facets of his days as a football coach at Carmel. When asked what he most remembered from that time, Coach Nyers told us, "I have never seen a community where the people were so engrossed with being champions." That one sentence emphasizes the spirit of the individuals described in this book and the spirit which continues to be a big part of what caused Carmel's "dot on the map" to become what it is today.

Mike Howard

Courtesy of 1967 CHS Pinnacle Yearbook

Introduction

Boasting just one stoplight, Carmel was a sleepy little farm town located approximately thirteen miles north of Indianapolis in the mid 1950's. Having a population of less than one thousand, Carmel at that time had no resemblance to the city of Carmel today! The downtown consisted of one bank, one hardware store, one theatre, and the "Toots" drive-in.

However, during that time, decisions were being made that would impact the destiny of the town forever. A new high school was being planned. Thus, a new basketball coach as well as a new football coach would be needed. These decisions helped to create a sports program unrivaled in Indiana sports history, which would become a model for sports programs around the Midwest and the country.

What follows are stories of the men and women who had visions and aspirations to make Carmel a town to be reckoned with. How did this remarkable series of events transpire in Carmel? No one suspected or sensed the seismic perfect storm brewing at Rangeline Road and Main Street in downtown Carmel. The necessary ingredients included a new high school, a young athletic director, two skilled coaches, and a few accomplished fathers to create Carmel Dads' Club.

This foundation laid in the '50s would lead to numerous individual state championship teams, national team championships, and national record setting winning streaks. Excellence in sports translated into excellence in the classrooms. Carmel High School has been recognized as a Blue Ribbon School. The Carmel Greyhounds Marching Band and the Ambassadors Show Choir set standards of excellence. Carmel High School is both envied and reviled. Success breeds contempt. Everyone circles the Carmel Greyhounds and considers beating them a major victory.

Carmel, Indiana is now a world renowned city famous for its roundabouts, bicycle and walking trails, and schools. As of 2014, Carmel High School has over 130 state championships in a variety of sports and is nationally ranked in girls' swimming. The district's schools consistently score well in state and national standardized tests. With a population of over 80,000, people see Carmel as a great place to raise and educate their children, and give them the opportunity to participate in various sports.

In 1959, however, Carmel's population was approximately 1,440, and a group of men sat around a kitchen table discussing their vision of what we now know as "Carmel Dads' Club." This compilation of individuals arrived on the scene from different backgrounds, in different careers and of varying ages. They had no idea their vision would have such an impact on the future quality of education, sports, music, and other programs offered to the residents of Carmel, Indiana.

1958 Sketch of Proposed New Carmel High School

Courtesy of CHS Dedication Ceremonies Program

November 9, 1958

Chapter One

Howard Wodock came to Carmel in 1953. After being a Navy Seabee in World War II, he played professional baseball in Pennsylvania. He later worked for the Nickel Plate Railroad in Ohio as an engineer. As his sons, Joe and Jack, started school, he began a new job in Indiana as a civil engineer with the Indiana Toll Road and was in charge of all the bridges. When the office was moved from Indianapolis to South Bend, Howard decided not to move his family again and instead went to work for the State Highway Commission. Thus, they stayed in Carmel. (Per conversation with Jack Wodock)

During the years before the Carmel Dads' Club, two men took different paths to become integral parts of summer youth baseball in Carmel. Howard Wodock was a parent who was interested in baseball for his sons and Dale Graham was anxious to have an opportunity to teach and coach at Carmel High School.

With the number of boys that wanted to play baseball, Howard was able to organize four teams of boys ages nine through eleven in a local house league that played on two fields on Main Street east of the old high school. He was disappointed in the conditions of these fields. There were no outfield fences and only small chain link backstops. After each game all the kids would line up and walk across the field picking up rocks. Howard coached one team, the Yankees. (Mrs. Wodock sewed "Y" on the ball caps for the boys on the team.) Mr. Russell Peek was Howard's assistant coach. Howard's teams were never less than runner up in the house league. During this time, Howard had two outstanding pitchers. Danny Reilley, his nephew, was imported to pitch for three years. The other pitcher was Rob Smith. (Rob later graduated from Carmel High School and is a retired Carmel Police officer.)

Howard was a stickler for the rules and was not opposed to getting into the umpires' faces during the games. According to Rob Smith, "Howard taught us boys how to play baseball *by* the rules as well."

Courtesy of Rob Smith

This picture shows Howard Wodock pitching. (The boys in the outfield are unidentified.) Howard was known to pull boys behind his car in during the winter on snowy days on a sled.

Carmel Little League Baseball 1961

Courtesy of Pete Davis

Cubs Baseball Coach is Mr. Davis. Boys include: **back row left to right:** Jim Pursel, Gary Runyon, Glen Ozols, Bill King, Loren Frisbie. **Front row:** Greg Hinshaw, Bob Cox, Tom McGoldrick, Bill Meeker, Renny Kline, and Pete Davis.

1965 County League Baseball

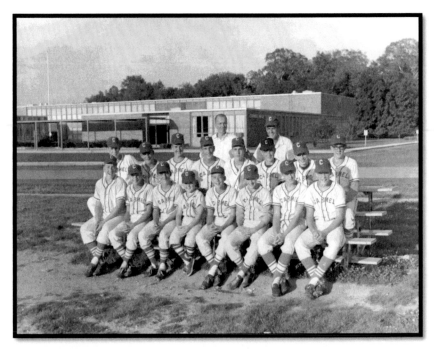

Courtesy of Pete Davis

Front Row left to right: Jim Pursel, Larry Lee, Chris Hadley, Mascot Jimmy Wodock, Pete Davis, Steve York, Doug Woods, and Dan Chapman. **Second row:** Norm Bristley, Mark McDonough, Geary Yost, Mike Ludlow, John McMahon, Steve Piersall, Sonny Sears, Mike Flohr. **Back row:** Mr. Flohr and Coach Wodock.

~

Dale Graham, his wife, Irma, and their three children were living in Gas City, Indiana in 1953. Dale was teaching 7th grade and coaching 7th and 8th grade track and basketball. Dale had attended Ball State and had become good friends with Dick Lamb. Dick was from Carmel, and was raised on his family farm down the road from St. Christopher's Episcopal Church on West Main Street. Dick called Dale and told him Carmel High School had an opening. Would he be interested in relocating? Dale jumped at the chance to teach at the high school level. The Grahams moved to Carmel in July of 1953. Dick and Elnora Lamb helped them move and get settled. Dale dove into his new job cleaning and organizing his area of the old high school. It took some time and effort as things were so disorganized and in such disarray. It is not what you know but sometimes who you know........

Just as Howard was establishing his baseball league, Dale was heading a summer baseball program for boys at the high school. He had the boys work on skills and play baseball games during the mornings and they went home for lunch. In the afternoon, Dale would drive a school bus and pick up the boys at their houses and take them to Northern Beach, a local swimming hole. As recalled by Irma, Dale's wife, one particular incident still upsets her to this day. "Dale had been instructed by the people at Northern Beach to not bring the two colored boys to swim there anymore. The next day, he stopped at their house and explained that he would not be able to take them. This was very troubling for Dale for years."

Summer Baseball 1963

Courtesy of 1963 CHS Pinnacle Yearbook

Coach Graham with team players: Rick Spencer, Jim Gaunt, Chuck Schaeffer, Larry Lewis, Paul Hannah, and Ken Kerchner.

Dale soon began overseeing athletics at Carmel High School. At the end of the summer of 1958, Howard spoke to Dale Graham regarding the poor conditions of the "lousy fields that are not suitable for a growing baseball league." The boys were still picking up rocks before and after the games and still had no outfield fences. Howard wanted better playing conditions for the boys. He truly felt that improved baseball fields would attract more players.

Dale became an effective icon managing athletics at Carmel. In September of 1958, the new high school was opened by Principal Olin Sweeney. Official dedication ceremonies were held on Sunday, November 9th. Somewhat disgruntled, Mr. Sweeney resigned in December of 1958. He drove to Vice Principal George Owens's house and dropped off his keys. Overnight, Earl Lemme became principal and Dale became the new Athletic Director of Carmel High School.

Carmel Elementary School was built in 1961. With the construction of this new school, opportunities were about to arise that would bring changes to the baseball diamonds in a dramatic fashion. Located south of Main Street and the new high school, it included unused school land. Dale and the Carmel School Board of Trustees made this land available as the future home of the fledging Carmel Dads' Club. Four baseball diamonds and one football field would be built on this ground. While Howard Wodock was working in South Bend, he came home on the weekends to spend time with his family. A natural leader and baseball enthusiast, Howard along with Neil Schmeltekopft and Jerry York, were about to turn these raw acres into fields of dreams. The four diamonds would be built around a small clubhouse/concession building and the football field would be on the far south east side of Carmel Elementary School. Lights were not affordable so all games would be played during daylight. Fences were also out of financial reach as well as dugouts at this time. Parking would be shared with Carmel Elementary School. The task was daunting but Howard Wodock, with his sons Joe and Jack in tow, worked each Saturday on the baseball fields. As Joe and Jack utilized the grade stakes, Howard surveyed all the 40 plus acres free of charge. Soon, new ball fields sprang up. Future Carmel High School athletes, Pete Davis, Dan Chapman, Mark McDonough, Steve York, Jim Pursel, and Dave Shepherd laid the sod for the diamond. At this time their ages ranged from nine to eleven.

Pete Davis at bat in 1969

In 1966 the first lighted field was designated for Howard's travel team. During this time, Carmel played travel ball against baseball teams from Cicero, Arcadia, Fishers, Noblesville, and other area teams. The baseball players won most of their games, local championships, and fed the Carmel High baseball program. All the boys who played for Howard said they learned more about baseball from him than any other coach they had during their careers. Mark McDonough, as a member of Howard's team, would hit home runs onto the roof of the new Carmel Elementary School. He continued to have a successful high school career and was "all state" in three sports. Others continued to play in high school as well and some even played college baseball as well. Pete Davis was a member of the baseball team at Arkansas State University that played in the Baseball Final Four Tournament for Arkansas State University in 1973.

Howard's passion and vision for baseball came from an outstanding career. He attended Penn State University where he played baseball and soccer. He was a captain on both teams. He played shortstop and third baseman. He played professionally in the AAA league. His vision and passion for baseball and coaching were two of his greatest core values. He taught his players not just how to play baseball but to do so by the rules. Howard passed away at the age of 51 in 1970 but his legacy lives on.

Baseball Sectional Champs

1967 1st IHSAA Tourney

Courtesy Pete Davis

This team was the fruition of all efforts to become the first Carmel baseball sectional win.

1st Row: Billy Shepherd, Brent Peek, David Hoemann, Jeff Newberg, Mark Egger, Joe Smith, **2nd Row:** Bill Marchal, John McMahon, Mike Gephart, Doak Baker, Norm Bristley, Pete Davis, Jerry Rockhill, Coach: Ron Adams, **Insert:** Geary Yost

Opening day of baseball in May, 1971, was declared Howard Wodock Day. Mrs. Dottie Wodock, widow of Howard, pulled the cord to show the new sign dedicating the Little League Fields behind Carmel Elementary School being named for Howard.

Indianapolis Star and News May, 1971

Those four fields that Howard helped bring to life behind Carmel Elementary School are named for him. Today, Wodock Field continues to be an active sports complex used by Carmel Dads' Club. This organization will forever be indebted to him for his capacity to organize and nurture Carmel Dads' Club baseball and to Dale Graham for assisting in the availability of the land that has allowed boys to enjoy playing baseball for decades.

~

Mr. Russell Peek showed his flair for writing in these poems he composed describing the players of the summer baseball teams of 1959 and 1960. They were donated by Rob Smith.

CARMEL YANKS OF '59

Under the bright and sunlit sky
In Carmel town one day,
They asked some boys to play some ball
Not fool around---just play!

They said, "You're Yankees now, you guys
You'll make mistakes, but then
We'll teach you how to do it right
And play like gentlemen."

And play they did--and how they played
They tried with all their might,
To hit, to bunt, to field the ball
And play the game just right.

He plays shortstop, old " Stovepipe" does
At pitching he's quite handy,
And at the bat he blasts them all
Don Riley is a dandy.

This boy, Joe Wodock, plays third base
He's quite a power hitter,
And though at times he swings like Sam
He never is a quitter.

This guy can play at first and on
The base paths really shines,
That's why they called him "Crazy Legs"
Yes, Dowty played real fine.

Whenever second "fluffed" a ball
His dad was on his back,
But when Steve Yeagley's at that plate
Just hear that big bat crack.

And "Fireball Smitty" has pursued
A very unique hobby,
He strikes out batters; one, two, three
Of course his name is Robbie.

This next guy caught and man like mad
And never griped at all,
And if that fly came to his field
Tom Townsend had the ball.

Who played as hard as any man
And ran so you could tell,
By the thudding of his flying feet
His name was Mike Cornell.

For just pure heart you couldn't beat
The Collins they called, "Small John",
When he was hit by a fast pitched ball
Delightedly yelled, "I'm on!"

Behind the plate he started slow
Just couldn't seem to move,
But when July came rolling round
Bruce Peek got in the groove.

The rest of these are lucky guys
They'll play this league some more,
When they start playing once again
Just hear that big crowd roar.

Who gave all he had and more
Who's there at every game,
Who watched the signals like a hawk
Pat Watkins was his name.

Who had a batting average of
650 and above,
Lee Schmidt, that's who, and better yet
He's magic with that glove.

Pat Beaver poled his two home runs
Then sickness stopped his bat,
But he'll be back to show them where
The home run fence is at.

At second, short, at field, at pitch
He's good-much better than many,
He's known as "Mr. Utility"
The Moran boy known as Kenny.

Chuck Johnson has improved this year
He's learned to bat and run,
With all the fellows on the team
He's had a lot of fun.

He'd play, and man he'd play real hard
He's trying all the time,
Jack Wodock digs like mad and runs
Five minutes on a dime.

"I'm safe, he's out, you're wrong."
                he'd yell
You'd think Brent Peek was dying,
He'd swing that bat and smack that ball
Always in there trying.

These are the Yanks, what did they do
To the teams that played baseball?
I'll tell you what, they're the Carmel
                              Champs
So bless them, one and all.

29

The runs are scored, the games are done
And who is on the top?
None other than that Yankee team
They're still the cream o' the crop.

Who are these guys who beat the best?
Who played the game so fine?
Well, step right up and meet the Yanks
We'll meet them all in line.

This lefty was a swifty guy
He'd win in any race,
Chuck Bristow would hit a ball 10 feet
And end up on third base.

The next man's not the biggest guy
His name is Benny Brown,
But with that cud of gum he'd chomp
And stare the pitchers down.

Ron Ehrgott came to us, and we
Were glad to see him play,
He hit when it would count the most
We wish that he could stay.

Who'd stand right up and take his out
And never tell the umpire off?
Because the umpire was his dad
The slugger man, Bill Goff.

Frank Guthrie mixed the pitchers up
They never saw the light,
You see he caught them lefty style
And yet he bats 'em right.

Send batters up, he'd mow 'em down
He'd drive those hitters screwy,
Who was this wizard with the ball?
No other than Mike Hughey.

That Hundley boy was slow at first
But, brother, he would try,
And toward the last our Terry boy
Had found his batting eye.

When Jack McCune would shake his head
We'd yell, "Nod up and down!"
He'd grin, rare back, and fire the ball
And stomp 'em in the ground.

Who stuck that long arm out at first
And hit the ball with ease?
The terror of the base path line
Bruce Peek hit when he pleased.

Brent Peek could bunt that ball just fine
His chatter's always breezy,
He'd gobble up those bouncing balls
And make the play look easy.

If only we could pitch this man
We'd never lose a game,
Without our Robbie Smith at short
We'll never be the same.

The Tiger team know this guy well
John Thomas is his name,
The Yanks were just one run ahead
His pitching won that game.

We need this guy in center field
He'll catch 'em, never fear,
Pat Watkins always gives his best
And grins from ear to ear.

Who was the catcher that could hit
The ball a country mile?
Mike Wilson hit the ball like it
Was going out of style.

While playing third, Jack Wedeck would
Sweat buckets full of water,
And could he hit, and could he run
Five minutes on a quarter.

For speed and power we're sure glad
Joe Wedeck's on our team,
He'd pass the bench so fast he'd make
Our drinking water steam!

A four run homer made Steve Wools
So proud he thought he'd burst,
He'd field a ball so fast he'd throw
A batter out at first.

Steve Yeagley made the hardest catch
Look easy when he played,
We missed his big and booming bat
We wish he could have stayed.

Well, there they are,—the Yanks,
                the champs,
They won again this fall,
They won because they were the best
They're YANKEES, one and all!

by Russ Peek

30

Chapter Two

As a few men in Carmel were beginning to focus on the sports program being offered in Carmel, two women were making a name for themselves as they were more interested in the quality of educating the children of Carmel. Anne Porteous and Jane Wilson became best friends while attending DePauw University in Greencastle, Indiana. Both women eventually moved to Carmel with their families. These mothers formed an official organization called "Better Schools Party." For such a little town, Carmel, with so much interest in the sports programs and now the school system, a perfect storm was brewing.

In 1955, the state of Indiana merged Clay Township and the section of Delaware Township east of the White River. With this merger, Carmel's population went from approximately 1,000 people to nearly 10,000 people. In 1956, Orchard Park Elementary School was built to help accommodate the increased population. This was the first school built in Carmel in 30 years.

Meanwhile, a group of concerned citizens, many new to Carmel, were interested in improving the quality of education for their children. Two of the leading couples were Anne and Al Porteous and Jane and John Wilson. Al grew up in Indianapolis, and attended First Presbyterian Church at 16th and Delaware Street. In the 1930's, the youth group from this church, including Al, would attend "get togethers" at William (Abe) Diddel's log cabin in Carmel. In 1945, after graduating from DePauw University, Anne moved to Indianapolis and began to attend First Presbyterian Church. Ann's landlord at 38th and Pennsylvania Street happened to be a good friend of Abe Diddel. Anne had worked as a blood chemist at Mayo Clinic after graduation. She moved to Indianapolis to work at Methodist Hospital.

Anne and Al began to date and eventually married. Abe had begun a new subdivision in Carmel surrounding a golf course with a private club called Woodland Country Club near his log cabin. Al and Anne purchased a lot on the 6th green and built their home. Meanwhile, John and Jane purchased a lot and built their home there against the advice of their family and friends. As best friends in college and now neighbors,

Anne and Jane set out to make an impact on this tiny rural town.

With the newly formed "Better Schools Party," these two women, along with Virginia Payne, proceeded to knock on every door of every voter in the Carmel area. Their ambitious goal was to form a Carmel school board. The "Better Schools Party" impacted the election of 1956 to the degree that local politicians, plus township trustee, Dan Stuckey, and influential citizens announced the organization of a school building corporation. Members of this board included Howard Hunt, President, John Gradle, Vice President, Ralph Baur, Secretary, and J. Warren Harvey, member of the Board of Directors.

But the town was divided on whether to renovate the old high school or build a new one. It was decided the people who wanted the new school, would have to purchase shares of stock at a price of $100 each into the school development corporation. There were sixty-eight original subscribers. Five hundred people eventually subscribed for a total of 762 shares of the corporation stock. $7,500 was raised with nearly 80% of the population in support of a new high school. With this money, 29 acres of land to the east of the old high school was purchased for new construction.

On December 5, 1956, the contract for constructing a new high school was signed. The new school was built at a cost of $1,594,919.92. Half of that cost was allocated for a new state of the art gymnasium with a seating capacity of 5,000. Many still questioned the rationale regarding building such a huge facility. The architecture firm of Vonnegut, Wright, and Porteous was given the contract to design and plan the high school. Al was the architect for the gymnasium. Construction of the new high school was completed on October 1, 1958.

Indianapolis Star Magazine, April 6, 1958

In the foreground the "old high school" can be seen. In the background, the construction of the new high school and the "state of the art" gymnasium continues.

Chapter Three

The phone rang. Most calls are not fortuitous but this one call would change the lives of many people in Carmel for generations to come. "Is Dick Nyers home?" asked Howard Hunt, a Carmel school trustee. The year was 1958 and it was a particularly hot summer in Ft. Leonard Wood, Missouri. Dick was in the process of completing a commitment to the Army. Dick replied, "Yes," and inquired what the call was about. Howard said that Carmel needed a new football coach. Ordinarily, that question would not raise an eyebrow and Dick stalled before inquiring about the coaching position. He had applied and had been turned down for the head basketball coach at Carmel and was told this in the same phone conversation. Who knew that momentous decision would have such an impact on Carmel High School's sports programs?

Dick Nyers attended Manual High School on the south side of Indianapolis. He was named to the All-City Teams in basketball, football, and baseball through his high school career. He also earned 13 varsity letters in 4 four sports while at Manual. Many Indianapolis sports writers considered Dick to be "the greatest all-around athlete in the history of Indianapolis." Dick continued to play football, basketball, baseball, and track at Indiana Central College now known as the University of Indianapolis. In his four years as a varsity football player, Indiana Central compiled a 24-9-1 record and three Hoosier Conference championships. By the time Dick graduated from college, he earned 14 letters in three sports. Dick continued to play football with the Baltimore Colts. By coincidence, he sat across from John Unitas on the airplane headed to Baltimore. Dick became one of John's favorite receivers. Dick was chosen to be on the travel squad during preseason and his job was to return kick-offs. He caught John's first preseason touchdown pass. He continued playing in the regular season at defensive safety and was chosen the Top Surprise of the 1956 Season. 1957 would be his final season to play professional football due to an injury.

~

During the Depression of the 1930's, the administration abolished football at Carmel High School. It wasn't until Waverly Myers was hired in 1951 with Dick Lamb as the assistant coach, did football make a comeback. The team's record was 4-2-1 that year. Incredibly, in 1952, the team compiled a record of 8-1-1. Unfortunately, that was also Coach Myers's last season with Carmel.

After some thought, on that hot summer day, Dick accepted the position on one condition. He would have complete control over the football program. Mr. Hunt assured him that would be the case. Though the new high school gymnasium was the main draw to bring in athletics, Dick would have the control of the vision for the football program at Carmel High School.

On July 10, 1958, Dick packed up all of his belongings and drove to Carmel. With practice starting August 15, Dick wasted no time. He rolled up his sleeves and went to work. His first order of business was to check out the CHS equipment. The uniforms were moldy, torn, and incomplete. No blocking equipment was to be found.

The second item was to transfer his half brother, Norm, "Pete," Bullard, from Manual High School in Indianapolis to Carmel High School. Pete, a junior and star athlete, moved in with Dick.

Courtesy of CHS 1961 Pinnacle Yearbook

Norm, "Pete," Bullard, Carmel High School,

Class of 1961

Facing an uphill struggle, next on Dick's list was to meet the football players. Twenty four young men, seventeen of whom were current football players came to the first meeting; only two were seniors. "The fact was that most our players were sophomores and juniors. We kept growing as a football team," said Dick Nyers.

Along with his assistant coaches, Don Huffer and Mel Sharp, Dick began to work with a group of players who were eager to please the new head coach. On the afternoon of September 1, 1958, the first football game under Coach Nyers was played at the new Carmel High School football field. Coach's first backfield consisted of Pete Bullard and Larry Breswick at halfback. Rick Davis was at fullback and Tad Sinnock was quarterback. Carmel defeated Sheridan 18-14. It was standing room only! To everyone's surprise, at the end of their first season together, they compiled a record of 5-5 with a team that only consisted of 29 players. Little did anyone realize that Coach Nyers was just getting started. He was a true visionary with an unparalleled work ethic and a strong desire to win.

1958 Carmel Varsity Football Team

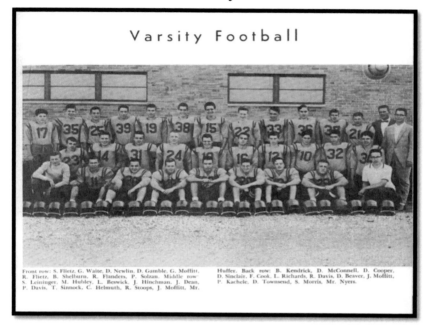

Courtesy of 1959 CHS Pinnacle Yearbook

Front Row: S. Flietz, G.Waite, D. Newlin, D. Gamble. G. Moffitt, R. Flietz, B. Shelburn, R. Flanders, P. Solzan, **Middle Row**: S. Leininger, M. Hubley, L. Beswick, J. Hinchman, J. Dean, P. Davis, T. Sinncok, C. Helmuth, R. Stoops, J. Moffitt, Mr. Huffer, **Back Row**: B. Kendrick, D. McConnell, D. Cooper, D. Sinclair, F. Cook, L. Richards, R. Davis, D. Beaver, J. Moffitt, P. Kachele, D. Townsend, S. Morris, and Mr. Nyers

41

During his first season as the football coach, Coach Nyers felt a feeder system was needed. This plan would be for boys in the fourth, fifth, and sixth grades. Then a junior high program for seventh and eighth grades would also be developed. Along with Dale Graham, Don Huffer would also become a part of this growing summer program.

~

Don Huffer grew up in Anderson, Indiana. He attended Franklin College and was drafted into the Army and was later shipped overseas to Korea. After returning from Korea, he graduated from Ball State University in 1957. He came to Carmel because he became acquainted with Dale Graham and Dick Lamb while at Ball State. In the fall of 1957, Don signed his teaching/coaching contract on a fence post on a farm located on West 116th Street. One of the trustees for Carmel Schools had a farm there and could not be in the trustee's office for this task as he was busy harvesting his crops. Don knew the new high school and gymnasium would be completed the following year and felt this was an *excellent opportunity. Not only was he an assistant football coach with Dick, he also helped with the summer baseball program along with Dale Graham and Tom Irvin. As Carmel Dads' Club was being organized, Dale became the President with Don as secretary. "We knew everybody in town. We knew the people. Don knew the kids and the parents," said Judy, Don's wife. "The money teachers received for teaching and coaching during the year ran out at the end of the year. So the coaches ran the summer morning programs for $500.00 each." (Per phone call with Judy Huffer)*

Dick also wanted to get the Our Lady of Mount Carmel (grades 1-8) football players interested in the Carmel High School program. His first strategy was to form the Carmel Dads' Club. This group, he reasoned, could handle the fourth, fifth, and sixth grades as well as the Carmel Pups (the best players from the Saturday morning program.) With the development of the Carmel Dads' Club, the junior high school would have a feeder system.

Then Dick brought together another piece of the puzzle. Soon after that first season was completed, Coach Nyers called his Manual buddies. This group of five men from Manual accepted his invitation to share his vision of a sports feeder system designed specifically to provide the necessary talent and skills to help build that powerhouse program he and Coach Bill Shepherd desired. The five men were Norm Bullard (Dick's father), Rex Fox, Bill Knapp, Elexer Vonpine, and Ted Bennett. Seven men from Carmel who also became a part of this vision and help ignite the sports program were Charles Hubley, Neil Schmeltekopf, Dick Helmuth, Roy Fleitz, Bill McMahan, Mr. Stanley, and Forrest Stoops. With all of these men on board, Coach Nyers began a start up football program that had boys in grades 4-6 playing football to eventually improve the football talent for a high school coach wired to win. Coach Nyers's second season as head football coach heralded a remarkable record of 7-2. Again, Pete Bullard, Larry Beswick, Rick Davis, and Tad Sinnock were members of that winning team. Coming on board as assistant coaches were Larry Goins, a lineman and All-American from Butler University, and Eric Clark, a Carmel High School graduate who as a four-sport athlete while attending Earlham College.

Winning can cause a lot of things to happen. The hope was that if the high school program was successful, the Our Lady of Mount Carmel football players would give

Carmel High School football a look. And they did! Dick also knew to utilize the move-ins. In 1958, Carmel had one young man join the team and in consecutive years, three or four new players joined the team as Carmel's population was growing rapidly at this time.

According to Dick, "I always met with the parents." I told them, "I'm coaching your sons. Go to church on Sundays. Your job is not to coach." Coach Nyers had rules for all the boys to follow and if they didn't, there were consequences. "Pete and Rick Davis, along with Mike Hubley, went to the Indiana State Fair one year. The boys knew they were all to be home by 10:00 pm. Unfortunately, they had a flat tire on the way home. The rule was if Coach Nyers called, you must answer the phone. Since none of the boys were home to do so, they had to run laps."

The results of this plan of a feeder system came to fruition during Dick's sixth and seventh seasons with records of 9-0-1 and 7-0-2, respectfully. "There was a period when we never lost in 19 games and that was with the first group that came through the Carmel Dads' Club program," said Dick. Carmel was engrossed with being a champion in basketball, but football developed faster. More sections of bleachers were needed to accommodate the spectators. "I have never seen a community come together as Carmel did at the football games. Everyone in town supported the team," said Dick. After Coach Nyers's second season the Carmel Dads' Club was now an entity.

Another huge boost to the Carmel High School football program was the formation of Carmel Dads' Club Pups. This was Coach Nyer's innovative idea of spring football. In 1962, he invited 8th grade boys with good academics to participate in spring football with the high school students. Bob Bowen, Dick Savidge, Mike Gephart, Jeff Newburgh, John Moran, and Jack Wodock were now a part of this program.

1961-62 Carmel High School Coaching Staff

Pictures courtesy 1961 Carmel l High School Pinnacle Yearbook

Left to right: Mr. Tom Irvin, Mr. Dick Nyers, Mr. Mel Sharp, Mr. Bill Shepherd, and Mr. Don Huffer.

Not only did Dick Nyers coach the football team, but he also coached the reserve basketball team during his time at Carmel High School. In the picture, Scott

47

McKinney aims for the basketball goal as Ford Wilson, Tom Warner, and Gene Hostetter prepare to go for the rebound.

Carmel Basketball B-Team 1963

Courtesy 1963 Carmel High School Pinnacle Yearbook

Team members: Tom Warner, Bruce Peek, Jim Mace, Ken Stephens, Dennis Dann, Lee Schmidt, Doug VonBurg, Gene Hostetter, Bill McCurdy, Jerry Merriam

Not pictured: Scott McKinney

Coach: Dick Nyers

Carmel was still a small town but under Dick's direction, the Greyhounds played a tough schedule. Carmel played bigger schools such as Lawrence Central and Warren Central, as well as North Central. Coach Nyers finished an outstanding career with two more winning seasons. In 1967, the Carmel Greyhounds finished the year with an 8-2 record. In 1968, they finished with a record of 7-3. Dick coached at Carmel from 1958-1968. His overall coaching career at Carmel High School was 77 wins, 26 losses, and 5 ties.

Dick Nyers—69 wins, 21 losses, and 5 ties.

1968 Coach Nyer's Final Season

Pictures Courtesy of 1968 CHS Pinnacle

Front Row: M. Egger, J.D. Clark, S. Gardner, M. Klingerman, R. Jacobs, M. Manien, S. York, R. Sumner, J. Russell, P. Weddington, B. McLean, **Second Row**: J. Russell, J. Moore, J. Purcel, D. Sales, S. McKinney, M. Flohr, P. Justad, R. Lane, K. Odom, M. Wood, S. Piersall, **Third Row:** W. Price, D. Smith, R. Doom, B. Irvin, G. Keasy, J. Wampler, B. Hubley, J. Zwisler, S. Wascoe, V. Tidman, W. Dunn, **Fourth Row**: D. Reeves, D. Sturtz, T. Blanford, C. Winkler, B. Park, P. Davis, W. Kline, **Back Row**: Coaches: R. Adams, R. Galloway, E. Clark, D. Nyers

~

In 1958 Carmel Clay Schools had just completed the new state of the art high school during this time. Half of the budget was dedicated to a basketball palace. This gymnasium was constructed where the spectators entered at ground level and walked down into the bleachers. With a seating capacity of 5,000 people, there was hope of hosting a sectional. And for such a tiny town to eventually host a basketball sectional was a mighty big dream for Carmel. Everyone in town, including Forrest Stoops, Carmel Clay Schools Superintendent, wondered how they would ever fill such a large gym. "I know a man in Mitchell, Indiana who can," said Dale Graham. Forest Stoops and school board member Howard Hunt drove to Mitchell and observed Coach Bill Shepherd in action. Coach Shepherd had been a star athlete at Butler University under Tony Hinkle and by the age of 29, he had already accrued three sectional wins. The School Board interviewed several candidates for the head basketball coaching position, including Dick Nyers. Bill was offered the position in 1957. Coincidentally, Edie, Bill's wife, had a brother, Don Cox, who was the construction supervisor *during the building of Carmel's new high school and gymnasium. Therefore, Bill and Edie were already quite aware of this extraordinary gymnasium being built.*

Coach Nyers and Coach Bill Shepherd, the newly hired basketball coach, shared many meals at Bill's home commiserating over their shared frustrations and mapping out a plan to transform Carmel athletics into a powerhouse. How would they turn a small high school with 315 students in grades 8-12 into a force to be reckoned with? There was not a large pool of talent from which to draw.

How fortunate for Carmel that destiny had brought Dick Nyers and Bill Shepherd together. Here were two young and talented coaches whose different paths aligned them in Carmel. They would become significant parts of the vision of excellence in sports that has since been achieved for decades. Carmel was now a powerhouse in many sports and there was no turning back.

Chapter Four

If 1958 was the vision year for the Carmel Dads' Club, 1959 was the organizational year. Led by Charles Hubley, a retired military man with an eye for detail, he had been in charge of a mess hall in Japan while in the Army. Coach Nyers brought the men from Manual High School to meet the men in Carmel. They began meeting regularly at the Hubley household sitting around the kitchen table to formulate and write the executive documents. (Charles Hubley notes).

Sitting around that kitchen table in the fall of 1958, were Dale Graham, Dick Helmuth, Bill Shepherd, Dick Nyers, Kevin Stanley, Paul Perralta, Don Huffer, Ray Fleizt, Ward Holm, and Neil Schmeltekopf. These men represented men who were parents of students attending Carmel High School as well as coaches and administrators. The original intent of this organization was primarily to support the high school athletic program and the students involved in these programs. Several meetings followed at St. Christopher's Episcopal Church on West Main Street. The Carmel community in general was very enthusiastic and supportive of these activities and the cause for which these men were directed. Even Forest Stoops, Carmel's school superintendent, attended some of these meetings. Members of Manual High School Dads' Club were asked to attend to help set up the organization. One member of that club, Mr. Elmer Von Pine, sales manager of the Banquet Milk Company, was very instrumental in helping with the organization of the Carmel Dads' Club. This being done, the first Board of Directors was elected to office:

- President- Charles Hubley
- Vice President- Kevin Stanley
- Secretary- Don Huffer
- Treasurer- Dick Helmuth
- Membership- Paul Perralta
- Finance Chairman- Joe Munson
- Athletic Chairman- Ray Fleizt
- Publicity Chairman- Ward Holm
- Ex Officio- Dale Graham
- Mason Officer- Henry Bracken

On March 9, 1959, Articles of Incorporation for the Carmel Dads' Club, Inc. were recorded with the Indiana Secretary of State. The names of the first CDC Board of Directors were made official. The names of the Incorporators were Charles Hubley, Kevin Stanley, Richard Helmuth, and Donald Huffer. The attorney who prepared all the legal documents was Phillip R. Correll, 1111 Audubon Drive, Carmel. (Phil later became Carmel's first Judge.) Don Huffer is the last surviving member of the first Board of Directors and Incorporators. (Charles Hubley's notes)

Within two or three years after this organization was established, it was apparent there was a need to not only support the high school level but also the grade school levels as well. There was one man who stood out in the organization, Neil Schmeltekopf, who incidentally was Carmel's railroad stationmaster. He was "the bed rock" of this organization and was the glue that held the Carmel Dads' Club together during the first ten years of its existence.

Other men were contacted for their support and effort in the background activities of the Dads' Club.

Namely:

- Mr. Russell Grant and Mr. Niles McMann, advertisement and promotion
- Mr. Walter Howard, concession operation
- Mr. Howard Wodock, grounds and facilities

"Some fifty years later we now have a super dads' club organization that comprises staff, facilities, and organization. Several athletic fields are presently being utilized and new facilities are on the drawing board. The current staff is dedicated to the very best programs and facilities possible and to maintain these standards comparable to the best in the country." (*Charles Hubley, Carmel Dads' Club Past President, 1959-1960*)

The following documents were provided by Bruce, Charles Hubley's son:

PHILIP R. CORRELL
ATTORNEY AT LAW
548 BANKERS TRUST BUILDING
INDIANAPOLIS 4

ME 4-4585

March 11, 1959

Mr. Charles Hubley
RR 2 Box 261BC
Carmel, Indiana

Dear Sir:

I am enclosing the certificate of incorporation for
CARMEL DADS' CLUB, INC., together with a copy of the Articles
of Incorporation, same showing the approval and filing with the Secretary of State and the recording with the Recorder of Hamilton County.

Also enclosed is my statement which includes the out of pocket
expenses for fees to the Secretary of State and to the Recorder.

I presume you will wish to turn these papers over to the Secretary and Treasurer respectively and if I can be of any further service,
such as the annual report about July 1, 1959, do not hesitate to call
upon me.

Very truly yours,

Philip R. Correll

prc:mw
encls.

A-1
(For use for Indiana Not for Profit Corporations.)
Form prescribed by the Secretary of State

— a —

ARTICLES OF INCORPORATION

of

CARMEL DAD S' CLUB, INC.

APPROVED
AND
FILED

MAR 9 1959

John B. Walsh
SECRETARY OF STATE OF INDIANA

The undersigned, being three or more natural persons of lawful age, at least a majority of whom are citizens of the United States, do hereby adopt the following Articles of Incorporation, representing beforehand to the Secretary of State of the State of Indiana and all persons whom it may concern, that a membership list or lists of the above named corporation for which certificate of incorporation is hereby applied for, have heretofore been opened in accordance with law and that at least three (3) persons have signed such membership list.

Be it further remembered that the following Articles of Incorporation and all matters heretofore done or hereafter to be done are in accordance with "An Act concerning domestic and foreign corporations not for profit, providing for fees, providing penalties for the violation thereof, and repealing certain laws," approved March 7, 1935, and all acts amendatory thereof and supplemental thereto.

1. The name of this corporation shall be **CARMEL DAD S' CLUB, INC.**

(Name must include the word "Corporation" or "Incorporated" or one of the abbreviations thereof.)

2. The purpose or purposes for which it is formed are as follows:

The purpose of this organization shall be to foster, develop and support the athletic program of Carmel High School and to promote favorable public relations between parents, faculty and community in regard to the athletic program.

3. The period during which it is to continue as a corporation is **perpetual** years.

4. The post office address of its principal office is **P.O. Box 314** Street,

  Carmel (City) **Hamilton** (County) **Indiana** (State)

5. The name of its resident agent is **Philip R. Correll**

6. The post office address of its resident agent is **111 Audubon Drive** Street,

  Carmel (City) **Hamilton** (County) **Indiana** (State)

7. If the memberships are to be divided into classes the designations of the different classes, and a statement of the relative rights, preferences, limitations and restrictions of each class, together with a statement as to the voting rights of any such class:

The membership is divided into two (2) classes, namely: Annual and Life.

Annual: A member of this classification has full voting rights for the year, as long as his dues are paid. The dues for this membership is $1.00 per member per year, payable in advance.

Life: A member of this classification has full voting rights as long as his dues are paid in full. The dues for this membership is $5.00 per member, payable in advance.

Neither the annual or life membership is transferable or assignable, and is not assessable.

— c —

8. The number of directors of this corporation shall be _____nine (9)_____ (This must be an exact number and cannot be stated in the alternative.)

9. The names and addresses of the first board of directors are as follows:

Name	Street	City	County	State
Charles Hubley	RR #2 Box 261BC	Carmel	Hamilton	Indiana
Kevin Stanley	13101 Thornhurst Dr. RR #2	Carmel	Hamilton	Indiana
Richard Helmuth	RR #1, Box 224	Carmel	Hamilton	Indiana
Donald L. Huffer	441 N. Range Line	Carmel	Hamilton	Indiana
Paul Peralta	13117 Thornhurst RR #2	Carmel	Hamilton	Indiana
Joseph H. Munson	10237 Central	Carmel	Hamilton	Indiana
Ray Fleitz	13103 N. College	Carmel	Hamilton	Indiana
Ward K. Holm	RR #1	Carmel	Hamilton	Indiana
Dale E. Graham	120 Third Ave. N.W.	Carmel	Hamilton	Indiana

10. The names and post office addresses of the incorporators are as follows:

Name	Street	City	County	State
Charles Hubley	RR #2, Box 261BC	Carmel	Hamilton	Indiana
Kevin Stanley	13101 Thornhurst Dr. RR #2	Carmel	Hamilton	Indiana
Richard Helmuth	RR #1, Box 224	Carmel	Hamilton	Indiana
Donald L. Huffer	441 N. Range Line Rd.	Carmel	Hamilton	Indiana

60

— d —

11. A statement of the property and an estimate of the value thereof, to be taken over by this corporation at or upon its incorporation:

    None

12. Any other provisions, consistent with the laws of this state, for the regulation and conduct of the affairs of this corporation, and creating, defining, limiting or regulating the powers of this corporation, of the directors or of the members or any class or classes of members:

    Each Director shall serve for a period of one year and until his
    successor is elected and qualified. Any vacancy occurring in the
    Board of Directors caused by death, resignation or otherwise, shall
    be filled by a majority vote of the remaining members of the Board.
    The Board of Directors shall consist of the President, Vice President,
    Secretary, and Treasurer of the organization and, in addition thereto,
    the five chairman of the standing committees as follows: Membership,
    Finance, Publicity, Committee on Athletics, and the Liaison Officer
    between this organization and the Triangle Club; the Athletic Director
    of the Carmel High School shall be considered an ex officio member of
    the Board of Directors. The full Board of Directors shall be necessary
    to constitute a quorum thereof, except for the filling of vacancies
    which shall require a majority of the existing Directors for a
    quorum; and the act of a majority of the Directors present at a meet-
    ing at which a quorum is present shall be the act of the Board of
    Directors.

— e —

Charles Hubley
Charles Hubley

Kevin Stanley
Kevin Stanley

Richard Helmuth
Richard Helmuth

Donald L. Huffer
Donald L. Huffer

A minimum of three of the incorporators designated in Article 10 on page — c — should sign above.

STATE OF INDIANA

COUNTY OF MARION }ss:

Before me, Philip R. Correll , a Notary Public in and for said County and State, personally appeared

Charles Hubley , Kevin Stanley

Richard Helmuth and Donald L. Huffer

(SEAL)

and severally acknowledged the execution of the foregoing articles of incorporation.

WITNESS my hand and notarial seal this

5th day of MARCH , 19 59

Philip R. Correll
Philip R. Correll Notary Public.

My commission expires April 15, 1962

(Articles of incorporation must be prepared in triplicate on the form prescribed by the Secretary of State, by the incorporators and signed and acknowledged by at least three of them before a Notary Public, and shall be presented in triplicate to the Secretary of State at his office accompanied by the fees prescribed by law.)

The above is a true copy recorded *March 11* 19 59.
Elizabeth Clover, Recorder Hamilton County.

62

335

Phil Council
1111 Andubare Dr.
Randolph

RECEIVED FOR RECORD

The ___11___ day of ___March___
A.D. _1957_ at ___ o'clock ___ M., and
recorded in papers ___54___ page _3-45-347_

Elizabeth Owen
Recorder Hamilton County

C O N S T I T U T I O N

CARMEL DAD'S CLUB

CARMEL HIGH SCHOOL

The undersigned, for the purpose of creating an organization among themselves in furtherance of the objects herein stated, at a meeting held in the St. Christopher's Episcopal Church, Carmel, Indiana, this 4th day of January, 1959, hereby establish the following Constitution.

ARTICLE I

NAME

The name of this organization shall be the Carmel Dad's Club of Carmel High School.

Carmel Dads' Club, Inc.

ARTICLE II

PURPOSE

The purpose of this organization shall be to foster, develop, and support the athletic program of Carmel High School, and to promote favorable public relations between faculty, parents, and community in regard to the athletic program.

ARTICLE III

MEETINGS

This organization shall meet once in each school semester within thirty days from the beginning thereof, and at such other times as may be specified by the executive committee.

ARTICLE IV

MEMBERSHIP

Any individual interested in furthering the athletic program of Carmel High School can become a member of this organization by signifying his intentions of becoming a member and paying the prescribed dues. The superintendent, principals, and members of the athletic department of the schools shall be considered members. (Non-paying).

ARTICLE V - OFFICERS

The officers of this organization shall consist of a president, vice president, a secretary and a treasurer, the duties of which shall be those which are customary in organizations of this character. The president, vice president and treasurer shall be fathers of high school pupils, but the secretary must be a member of the staff of the school. Said officers shall hold their respective offices until the May meeting, (the month of May is set forth as the month when a stated meeting

64

will be held to elect new officers), or until their successors shall be elected. Vacancies occurring between meetings shall be filled by the executive committee. At the first meeting of the second semester, the president and athletic director, jointly, shall appoint a nominating committee, consisting of five members of the organization. Said committee shall meet sometime beforethe month of May following their appointment. And they shall nominate one member for each of the offices of the organization and report such nominations at the May meeting of the organization. Other nominations may be made from the floor at such meeting, and a separate secret ballot shall be taken in all cases where there is more than one nomination for any office.

ARTICLE VI

STANDING COMMITTEES

There shall be the following standing committees consisting in each case of a chairman, who shall be appointed by a majority of the elected officers and such other members as may be selected by said chairman with the advice and consent of the president.

(1) A membership committee - to promote and increase the membership of this organization.

(2) A finance committee - to foster, develop and promote ideas and events which will increase the financial status of this organization.

(3) A publicity committee - to supervise publicity and further amicable relations with the public generally and such organizations as have an interest in furthering the development of the school athletic program.

(4) A committee on athletics - to work with the several coaches of the athletic teams and render such encouragement and assistance in athletics as may, to said coaches, seem proper.

(5) A liaison officer - shall be one member appointed by the Triangle Club of the school in such manner as they shall deem proper, and who shall meet with the executive committee in an advisory capacity to assist in directing the activities of the organization in such manner as to avoid conflict with the activities of the Triangle Club and its several committees.

Additional committees may be created by a majority action of the executive committee.

ARTICLE VII - EXECUTIVE COMMITTEE

An executive committee is hereby created consisting of the president, vice president, secretary, treasurer, and the chairmen of the standing committees which shall be vested with full authority to act for the organization between stated meetings. The athletic director shall be considered an ex-officio member of the executive committee.

65

ARTICLE VIII

DUES

The dues of this organization shall be $1.00 per member, per year, payable in advance. A lifetime membership can be had by payment of $5.00 in advance.

ARTICLE IX

AMENDMENT

The Constitution can be amended by three-fourths (3/4) majority of a quorum being present.

ARTICLE X - QUORUM

A quorum shall be fifteen percent (15%) of the total membership.

ARTICLE XI

INOPERATIVE ORGANIZATION

In the event of the extinction or the depletion of this organization - all existing assets will be turned over to the principal of Carmel High School to be used in furthering the athletic program. This organization shall be deemed inoperative if no stated meetings are held in any given calendar year.

— c —

Charles Hubley
Charles Hubley

Kevin Stanley
Kevin Stanley

Richard Helmuth
Richard Helmuth

Donald L. Huffer
Donald L. Huffer

A minimum of three of the incorporators designated in Article 10 on page — c — should sign above.

STATE OF INDIANA

COUNTY OF............MARION............}ss:

Before me, ...Philip R. Correll..., a Notary Public in and for said County and State, personally appeared

............Charles Hubley..., Kevin Stanley............

............Richard Helmuth and Donald L. Huffer............

(SEAL)

and severally acknowledged the execution of the fore-going articles of incorporation.

WITNESS my hand and notarial seal this............

5th day of MARCH , 19 59

Philip R. Correll
Philip R. Correll   Notary Public.

My commission expires............April 15, 1962

(Articles of incorporation must be prepared in triplicate on the form prescribed by the Secretary of State, by the incorporators and signed and acknowledged by at least three of them before a Notary Public, and shall be presented in triplicate to the Secretary of State at his office accompanied by the fees prescribed by law.)

The above is a true copy recorded *March 11* 19 59.
Elizabeth Clover, Recorder Hamilton County.

The
Carmel Dads Club

IN
GREATFUL RECOGNITION

Of services above and beyond the requirements of good citizenship in organization and leadership, as the first president and in stirring the hearts and efforts of your fellow men to make the Carmel area a better place in which to live and to raise tomorrow's leaders, "our children" hereby, this 22nd day of May 1959, bestows this public acknowledgement upon

Charles B. Hubley

CARMEL
DAD'S CLUB

"HELPER BUDDIES OF TOMORROWS LEADERS"

VICE PRESIDENT
TREASURER
SECRETARY
MEMBERSHIP CHAIRMAN
FINANCE CHAIRMAN
ATLETIC CHAIRMAN
PUBLICITY CHAIRMAN

1961 Carmel School Board

Courtesy of 1961 Carmel High School Pinnacle Yearbook

Members of the 1961 School Board included: Don Fry, Kenneth Booth, Forest M. Stoops (Clay Township Schools Superintendent), Jack Shore, Ward Holm, and Howard Hunt. Several of these men were also an integral piece of the establishment of the Carmel Dads' Club. Fathers, educators, coaches and business men who came together to improve educational and athletic opportunities for Carmel's youth.

Chapter Five

At the end of World War II, when many men were returning to college and wanted to play football, Jerry York started the first football team in Indiana with players who had played before going into the service. This team was founded, coached, and managed as a semi-professional football team which won the 1946 State Championship. Their opposing teams were unable to score against them. The following year, 7-UP Bottling Company became the sponsor and they were known as the 7-UP All Stars. Sponsorship ended after a couple of years. In 1949, the team had no sponsor and dressed in Jerry's basement. Having no money, on Monday mornings the uniforms were hung on the clothesline and Mrs. York beat them clean with a broom. All games were played away as they could not pay another team to come to Indianapolis. Then a miracle happened:

A man named Tryon Chekoff called and was interested in purchasing the team. So Jerry sold the team and all the equipment for a few hundred dollars. As a Westside bar owner, Mr. Chekoff had dreamed of owning a football team. The team became known as the Tryon All Stars. It was the first professional football team in Indianapolis. Jerry York became the manager of this team; this was part of the purchase agreement. The Tryon All Stars had the highest per game payroll of any professional sport in Indianapolis at the time. Jerry handled the hiring, scheduling, promoting, and all miscellaneous activities with the exception of coaching. They had a 12 game winning season and a state professional championship in 1949. Home games were played on the CYO field in Indianapolis. Incidentally, they were the only football team in the United States that had all their games televised. On Saturday evenings, Jerry was on a television sports program discussing the team and various players. Mr. Chekoff continued with the team but after three years could no longer afford it. Jerry resigned from the team to devote full time to his insurance business until his son, Steve, started playing little league football at Tabernacle Presbyterian Church and then at Carmel.

Then in June, 1956, Jerry and Peggy York were contacted by John Kitchen, an attorney for the Lilly Foundation. The Yorks were not really interested in moving to Carmel because they already had a successful kindergarten operating in Indianapolis on Washington Boulevard, across the street from Tab. However, they made an offer of $20,000 for 6 1/2 acres, a farm house, a school building, a tennis court, and assorted school materials on Smokey Row Road at 136th Street. Their offer was accepted. Additional land (24 1/2 acres) was purchased from Mrs. Purdy, original owner of all the land. She and her husband, a former Vice President of the Marmon Car Company, used the Carmel property as a summer vacation home. During this time, Jerry's love and knowledge of football was rejuvenated. He became the first coach of the Carmel Pups and continued in this role for five years. (Mrs. Peggy York)

Jerry built a sports legacy at Tabernacle Presbyterian Church in Indianapolis. He was also president of the recreational program at Tab which happened to be the largest church youth program in the United States. Their fourth child and only son, Steve, began playing football at the age of six at Tab. Jerry's nephew, Noby, the same age as Steve, played football for Tab and soon was living with Jerry and Peg in Carmel during the summers. Dick Nyers called Jerry in 1958 and asked him to leave Tab and take on the challenge of starting a similar football program in Carmel with the Dads' Club. In 1959, Jerry was coaching both teams at Tab and Carmel with Steve also playing for both teams. At this time, Carmel did not have a field for youth football. Since he was helping Howard Wodock build the baseball diamonds behind Carmel Elementary School, he believed that a football field could be built on the southeast side of the school. The town of Carmel did not feel there was enough room there for a football field but Jerry pressed on. He needed a 35 ft. strip of land and acquired it from the adjoining land owner. It was a piece of land in a vacant field that would later become Concord Village. With enough land in hand, Jerry built a football field with his personal collection of two goal posts and eleven yard markers. This was the beginning of Carmel Dads' Club youth football program.

Carmel Pups Football Team 1962

Courtesy of Mike Easterday

Coaches: York, Ivy, and Richards, Stephenson, Sturtz

Players: **Back Row:** Tony Faust, Dean Ransom, Tom McMillan, Bob Giles, Pete Holm, Brad Rice **Middle Row:** Mark Ivy, Carl Winkler, name unknown, Stan Wade, Randy Reahard, J.D. Blake, Bruce Hancock, Bob Wright, Lester Rainey, Don Sturtz, Steve Wilson **Front Row:** John Slough, Bob Cox, Gary Stephenson, Scott Richards, Jim Wodock, (mascot) Bill Gardner, Pete Davis, Ancel Bell, Roger Fox

Since the high school team was the Greyhounds, the coaches named this new team the Carmel Pups. The team began playing games in 1960. The schedule was ambitious and included such teams as the Deaf School, Arlington, Speedway, and Bloomington. The Pups were undefeated in 1963. Because of all the team's success, Coach York was prompted to contact the Milk Bowl representatives in McKeesport, Pennsylvania outside Pittsburgh. The game was billed as a national championship game. The Dads' Club and the Carmel Pups had gone national. Though the age limit of the players was 12 and the weight limit was 118 pounds, the Pups were allowed to bring five 13 year olds along for the game. Steve York, Noby York, Pete Davis made the trip. Unfortunately, the Pups lost 42-13, but a legacy was established.

1963 Milk Bowl Team

Courtesy of Dan Chapman

Front Row: No.15 Bruce Hancock, No.28, Stan Wade, No.12, Pete Davis, No.11 Gary Stephenson, No.35 Jimmy Wodock (mascot), No.16 Roger Fox, No.13 Scott Richards, No.14 J.D. Blake, No.25 Carl Winkler

Second Row: No.17 Pete Holm, No.27 Bobby Giles, No.22 Bobby Cox, No.21 Randy Reahard, No.18 Gary Lovingfoss, No.19 Don Sturtz, No.20 Lester Rainey, No.23 Dean Bell, No.29 Bobby Wright, No.32 Mark Ivy, No.33 Brad Rice

Back Row: Coach York, Mr. Stephenson, Mr. Sturtz, No.31 Dan Chapman, No.26 Tom McMillan, No.34 Tony Faust, No.30 John Slough, No.24 Dean Ransom, Mr. Ivy, Mr. Richards, Mr. Schmeltekopft

1963 Pups Awards Banquet

Courtesy of Dan Chapman

Mr. Jerry York is shown presenting a trophy to Noby York along with Dan Chapman and Pete Davis.

Jim Sturtz became head coach of the Pups in 1964. The four years' record of the first Carmel Pups team was 32 wins, 4 losses, and 3 ties. (But after that, the team had a number of years where it was undefeated with 76 wins and 0 losses.) The payoff was felt immediately at the high school level as the players progressed through school. The players who were on the original 1960 Pups team were now freshmen. Coach Nyers asked two of those players, Jack Wodock and Mike Gephart, to play up on the varsity football team at Carmel High School. After two mediocre years of football with average players, 1961's varsity team had a record of 5-4-1. In 1962 the record improved to 6-4. In 1963 the record was 8-2, in 1964, it was 9-0, 1965 the record was 7-0-2, and in 1966 the varsity team had a record of 8-2. The Pups' influence was realized. Dick Nyers' vision had become a reality.

Chapter Six

Thomas Hugh Irvin was born August 10, 1922 in Hagan, Virginia. His father was a farmer and a coal miner and from 1948 to 1956 he was also a jailer and deputy sheriff in Lee County, Virginia. Tom attended a one-room school in Hagan. He lettered in basketball and baseball and graduated from Flatwoods High School in 1941. Tom later returned to Hagan to teach at the same elementary school he attended as a young boy. He attended Lincoln Memorial University from 1941-1942, while working on the LMU farm for twenty cents an hour to help pay college expenses. Drafted into the military in 1942, Tom served in North Africa, Sicily, and Italy during World War II. He returned to LMU after completing his military service and earned a B.A. degree. He served as a teacher, coach, and principal in Lee County from 1947-1957. In 1957 he and his family moved to Noblesville, Indiana and continued teaching and coaching. Tom supervised the Boys Club in Noblesville during the evenings and attended Ball State University and completed his Masters Degree.

In 1960, he and his family moved to Carmel to begin twenty- five years of a remarkable career with Carmel Clay Schools and be an integral part of the formation of the Carmel Dads' Club. As Tom began his career in Carmel, he taught junior high math. Later, he would become Assistant Principal under George Owens at Carmel Junior High School. He was head baseball coach at the high school as well as the freshman basketball coach. At the time, the baseball field was located behind the high school and was in terrible condition. He would drag old wire fencing behind his car, a 1955 Buick Special, across the field as members of the baseball team would pick up rocks before the games and practice. (Toots Irvin, Tom's wife)

On a cold March day in 1961, Carmel Elementary School opened its doors with Tom Irvin as its principal. Students were transported on buses to Carmel Elementary School from Orchard Park Elementary School while the other students walked across the street with their books and supplies in hand from the "old high school." A class of fourth graders being taught by Mrs. Phyllis Rockhill at the old Friends Church on North Rangeline Road also made the trek to Carmel Elementary School that day. For most of the students, this was their first experience in a brand new building. It was an adventure that many of the students still remember today. Carmel Elementary School would play an integral part of the formation and success of Carmel Dads' Club.

Carmel Elementary School April, 1966

Courtesy of Bob Irvin

Three baseball diamonds and the Pups Football field can be seen in this aerial view of Carmel Elementary School. The concession stand is also visible.

A major concern for Carmel High at this time was being able to afford, attract, and keep great, young coaches. The "Morning Program" was brought to Carmel by

81

Coach Bill Shepherd who had used a similar program in Mitchell, Indiana. A stipend of $500 per summer was paid to Dick Nyers, Dale Graham, Don Huffer, and Bill. The program was designed to keep young athletes active during the summers as well as offset the fact that teachers and coaches were not paid during the summer months. At the same time, a Saturday morning basketball league was keeping the new high school gym occupied. The new gym had the ability to make two courts available for simultaneous play as side baskets could be rolled down. This league also filled up the gymnasium in the old high school as well as the gymnasiums in both the new Carmel Elementary School and Orchard Park Elementary School. EmRoe Sporting Goods provided the needed equipment.

The young athletes purchased their own jerseys, shorts, and socks. The next year, the athletes sold their jerseys to the next year's group of athletes. Approximately 100 boys, ages nine through twelve, began to sign up annually to play summer basketball, which created a feeder system for talent for the future of Carmel High School basketball. Organized basketball games were played in the new high school gymnasium. Soon interest developed and a travel team was organized. Games were scheduled around Hamilton County.

1961 Carmel Eagles Little League Basketball Team

Courtesy of Pete Davis

Front Row: Pete Holm, Mike McCurdy, Dave Shepherd, Dave Walton, Bob Cox

Back Row: Mr. Mace, Pete Davis, Don Currise, Jay Mace, Mr. Currise

In the spring of 1963, a new teacher and basketball coach was hired. Fresh out of Butler University and raring to go, Tom Meeks was handed the responsibility of staffing and running a Saturday morning basketball program. Tom met with Carmel Dads' Club coaches as well as Neil Schmeltekopf. Each Saturday morning, he opened five gyms and made sure basketballs and scorebooks were at each venue. He hired high school basketball players and paid them each $5.00 to referee two games. Tom assessed all participants on dribbling, shooting layouts, and free throws. For all of his efforts, Tom Meeks was paid $200.00.

The tight schedule ran like clockwork with Tom's steady hand and management skills. Practice was 8:00 am to 9:00 am with games 9:00 am to 10:00 am. Another hour of practice followed along with games until noon. It was a frenetic sight but the feeder system had begun. After the last games were played, Tom collected the balls, the scorebooks, paid officials, and locked the gymnasiums. At home he compiled all the statistics and printed the results. This was a good day until Monday morning when Tom Irvin would call Tom Meeks to complain about the condition of the gymnasium at Carmel Elementary School after the weekend's activity. One time, Tom paid Mr. Irvin

$200.00 for some damage done at the gym at the elementary School.

During the summer of 1963, David Shepherd, age 11, led the summer league with 373 points followed by Dan Chapman with 93 points. The championship was won that summer by the team that included Rodney Doom, Pete Holm, and Don Currise, defeating Dave Shepherd's team.

Throughout this time during the morning basketball program, there were no drills, no zone defense, or pressing. The "Butler Way" was being used by all the coaches. Coach Shepherd was now using it at the high school. Tom Meeks was also using it with the 7th and 8th grade basketball teams as well. With a combined two year record of 35-1, the results were immediate and amazing. These wins are assumed to be accurate but the one loss is verified. Tom Meeks coached until 1970, culminating an approximate record of 100-5 in 7 years.

1965 Carmel Junior High

7th Grade Basketball Team

Courtesy of Mike Easterday

Coaches: Tom Meeks and Greg Fearrin, **Players**: Dave Shepherd, Randy Carter, Don Currise, Randy Ludlow, Pete Holm, Dan Chapman, Rodney Doom, Mark McDonough, Brad Rice, Doug Rafferty, Tom Thornberry, Dean Ransom, Pete Porteous

Courtesy of Bob Irvin

PTO members Mrs. Al Porteous, Mr. John Hensel, Mrs. Robert Jackson, and Mrs. Curtis Stumm present a check to Mr. Tom Irvin from proceeds of a PTO sponsored art fair to purchase books for the Carmel Elementary School library in May, 1967.

As the decade of the 1960's rolled along, basketball at both the high school and junior high levels began to develop. The Carmel High School Athletic Department was now headed by Bill Shepherd. The basketball teams at the high school level were evolving into strong teams. In 1965-66, Billy Shepherd, Bill's oldest son and a product of the Carmel Dads' Club, along with the other members of the Carmel Varsity Basketball Team, won Carmel's first basketball sectional title in 45 years, beating Noblesville. With just seconds left in the game, Billy drilled the ball just inside the half court line to win the game!

Other sports at Carmel High School were beginning to feel the effect of the feeder system. Also in 1966, two State Wrestling Champions were crowned from Carmel; Dick Savidge and Larry Smith. In 1968, Carmel's basketball team led by Billy and Dave Shepherd, both products of Carmel Dads' Club, enjoyed a regular season record of 21-3. (Carmel lost in the regional to the eventual state runner up, Marion High School.) The team was undefeated in 1969 and Dave led Carmel to a State runner up finish in 1970. Billy and Dave were honored as Mr. Basketball in 1968 and 1970. Both boys also enjoyed tremendous college careers and Billy played professional basketball as well.

The Carmel Varsity Basketball team won its first Sectional in 1966 and continued to win the 1967 and 1968 Sectionals. Many of these boys had played basketball with Coach Meeks at Carmel Junior High School and had been a part of the Saturday Morning Program as well. These Sectional winners truly were the fruition of all the efforts to attain that first win and many more Sectional and eventual State wins for years to come.

1968 Carmel Basketball Sectional Winning Team

Front Row: T. McGoldrick, C. Evans, S. York, S. Richards, D. Shepherd, B. Shepard. Second Row: Asst. Coach Eric Clark, Manager B Marchal, N. Bristly, T. Schmidt, D. Ransom, M. Ludlow, G. DeSmet, Manager B. Meeker, Head Coach Bill Shepherd.

Courtesy of Carmel High School 1968 Pinnacle Yearbook

Front Row: T. McGoldrick, C. Evans, S. York, S. Richards, D. Shepherd, B. Shepherd, **Second Row**: Asst. Coach Eric Clark, Manager B. Marchal, N. Bristley, T. Schmidt, D. Ransom, M. Ludlow, G. DeSmet, Manager B. Meeker, Head Coach Bill Shepherd

Courtesy of 1967 Carmel High School Pinnacle Yearbook

Coach Dick Nyers is given a service award by Owen Park, President of the Carmel Dads' Club, at the end of the 1967 basketball season. Dick was the driving force that visualized and brought together the men who formalized the organization known as the Carmel Dads' Club.

90

1970 Mr. Basketball of Indiana

Courtesy of Mike Easterday

1970 Mr. Basketball of Indiana

Indianapolis Sunday STAR Magazine June 14, 1970

The Carmel golf team won the State Championship in 1970. The team was coached by Don Huffer, an original member of the Board of Directors of Carmel Dads' Club. Don Currise, Russ Craig, Doc O'Neal, and Pete Holm were a force to be reckoned with on this team. (Coincidentally, his father, Ward, was a member of the first Carmel School Board.)

1970 Golf County and Conference Winners

Row one: R. Craig, B. Wright, D. O'Neal, B. Yde, D. Currise. Row two: Coach Don Huffer, G. Duke, S. Hixon, S. Norris, P. Holm, B. Gardener, Coach Ray McDonald.

Courtesy of 1970 Carmel High School Pinnacle Yearbook

Row one: R. Craig, B. Wright, D. O'Neal, B. Yde, D. Currise **Row two**: Coach Don Huffer, G. Duke, S. Hixon, S. Norris, P. Holm, B. Gardner, Coach Ray McDonald

Also in 1970, Tom Irvin became Assistant Superintendent of Carmel Clay Schools after serving a year as Director of Curriculum. He also served as Director of Personnel for the district. (Dr. Irvin retired in 1985. He passed away in 2003.)

As Carmel moved into the 70's and beyond, new schools were built. As Carmel's population grew, so did the enrollment in Carmel Clay Schools. It now has approximately 16,000 students. The high school has become the largest high school in the state with an enrollment exceeding 4,800. It has been remodeled and expanded several times. A new football stadium was constructed on 40 acres in 1994. Four gyms and an Olympic-sized swimming pool have been added to the original gymnasium. A new baseball field, Hartman Field, was constructed in 1995. In 2014, a new weight training facility was added.

The Carmel Dads' Club did not stand pat. They grew from four original baseball fields and one football field to several sports complexes and a permanent administrative building. Today, Carmel Dads' Club manages four sports: football, baseball, basketball, and soccer and participation by both boys and girls exceed 13,000. The feeder system is an indisputable success. As of 2013, Carmel High School boasts over 125 team championships and 220 individual champions, according to Jim Inskeep, Athletic Director of Carmel High School. A person would have to go back to 1983-1984 to find a year when Carmel did not win a State championship. The girls' high school swim team won the first State championship 27 years ago, has never lost the state title in those 27 years and is ranked nationally.

The Carmel Dads' Club is the gold standard for youth sports programs in the United States. The legacy of Dick Nyers is played out as other schools across the nation try to develop sports programs to emulate the programs we have in Carmel today.

Thank you, Coach Dick Nyers, for acting on your convictions and vision. Thanks to Neil, Jerry, and Howard for making the vision a reality through the Carmel Dads' Club. You all are iconic figures in the annals of Carmel's sports history. You helped to make Carmel's dot on the map larger and become a force to be reckoned with in many sports, including football, basketball, tennis, wrestling, soccer to name a few. Howard Wodock, Jerry York, and Neil Schmeltkopf worked tirelessly to build fields, fund programs, and coach winning teams. They each left an indelible mark on thousands of young athletes. Because of people like Dale Graham, Bill Shepherd, and the staff at Carmel

High School, students are encouraged to excel in an environment in all fields whether it is academics, sports, or the performing arts departments. Finally, to Anne Porteous, who set the wheels in motion by forming the Better School Party. She pulled the small town of Carmel up by its collective bootstraps and willed a new high school into existence – and the thousands of volunteers who preceded her and made it possible. "Behind the men were the women who supported the men," said Anne Porteous.

"But as in all organizations, we often lose sight of the efforts and courage of the founders of the organization in the early years. The initial organizers of youth sports and the Carmel Dads' Club, like those who initiate any activity, have two universally common characteristics. First they have no idea how the movement will evolve or even if it will succeed. Secondly, if successful, the founders move forward with energy, dedication, and perseverance to lay the foundation for the future," (Mike Howard.)

CONCLUSION

By

Pam Shepherd Otten

In July of 1957, my parents drove my sister and me, along with our very carsick beagle, from Lawrence to Carmel and settled in to the Auman Addition. We quickly made new friends, roamed the neighborhood, and enjoyed feeding the calves in the pasture. We rode our bikes "uptown" to the library to check out books (the children's section was located where Woody's Bar is today.) We stopped at the Trend Shop on West Main Street to purchase penny candy. I attended kindergarten in the Lions' Club on East Main Street. Our neighborhood attended elementary school at the "old" high school which housed grades 1-12. But for some reason, we seemed to get tossed between attending "Old North" or Orchard Park Elementary School on a yearly basis. We would invariably start at one school and in a few weeks we would be transferred to the other school until our parents collectively "put their feet down." In March of 1961, my sister and I were among the students at Orchard Park who gathered books and supplies in grocery sacks and boarded buses to become students at Carmel Elementary School. I can still visualize the students walking across Main Street from Old North with their sacks of books and supplies in hand.

Auman Addition 1958

Indianapolis Sunday Star Magazine, April 6, 1958

We lived at 1024 East Auman Drive which was across the street from the barn in the forefront of the picture on the preceding page. Today Mohawk Hills Apartments are located where the farm was. We moved to a larger home in Johnson Addition on West Main Street in 1962. We played outside until dinner time and roamed the fields where Wilson Village exists. It was here where I became associated with many of the people mentioned in this book. We played kickball or "four square" in the streets or sat next to one another in class. As a teenager I babysat for Coach Nyers' young children. Growing up attending Carmel schools many of the coaches were my teachers. Mr. Graham and his family lived around the corner. Mr. Meeks was my science teacher and neighbor and teased me as I practiced baton twirling in the backyard. I gave baton twirling lessons to Mr. Huffer's daughters who lived in the neighborhood. I had Mr. Huffer for a business class in high school. He and Mr. Clark were my driving instructors during the summer of 1968. Coach Nyers was also a driving instructor and would let my best friend and me drive home from summer school each day. One hot afternoon, he and I picked up my neighbor's garbage after my best friend, who shall remain nameless, knocked over their trash cans while backing out of my driveway! My perspective of the coaches was entirely different than how the athletes viewed them. They were neighbors, family men, and teachers.

At the time, I was not aware of the dynamics of the sports programs at the schools or through the Carmel Dads' Club. I knew the boys played baseball during the summers because I worked one summer at the Dairy Queen and the teams came in for ice cream after the games. My father, Ray Farmer, sponsored many Carmel Dads' Club baseball teams through his business, The Carmel Car Clinic, and would buy the teams ice cream after each game, whether they won or lost.

As a member of both the Carmel Marching Greyhounds and the cheer block, I attended all of the football and basketball games during the late 1960's and in 1970 when I graduated. We cheered for Steve York, Pete Davis, Dan Chapman, and the rest of the football team. We watched Billy and Dave Shepherd and others players such as Dean Ransom make history during the basketball seasons.

1970 Number 2 in State!

Back row: D. Graham, D. Wilson, D. Scott, G. Cline, S. Wilson, D. Ransom, R. Ludlow, Coach Clark, B. Thornberry, Coach Shepherd, R. Rahke. Second row: G. Duke, S. Odom, J. Gradle, G. Duryea, B. Yde, D. Shepherd. Front row: G. Hoopingarner, W. Rogers, C. Black, D. Clark, S. Shepherd, C. Polley, D. Clark.

Courtesy of 1970 CHS Pinnacle Yearbook

Back Row: D. Graham, D. Wilson, D. Scott, G. Cline, S. Wilson, D. Ransom, R. Ludlow, Coach Clark, B. Thornberry, Coach Shepherd, R. Rahke, **Second Row**: G. Duke, S. Odom, J. Gradle, G. Duryea, B. Yde, D. Shepherd, **Front Row**: G. Hoopingarner, W. Rogers, C. Black, D. Clark, S. Shepherd, C.Polley, D. Clark

The feeder system started nearly decade earlier was paying off. Many of these players on this team played on several Carmel Dads' Club sports teams as young boys. Carmel was now on its way to becoming a strong contender, not only in basketball and football, but other sports as well.

After graduation from Ball State University, Dr. Irvin hired me as a third grade teacher at Carmel Elementary School. Here I was, a new teacher at the very school I attended as a child, spent one semester as a senior in high school cadet teaching and where I was a BSU student teacher. With so many varied experiences in this school, it was especially meaningful to have my own class at Carmel Elementary School. As I began teaching in the fall of 1974, my loyalty to Carmel Elementary deepened. I was completely vested in this school system.

My own children attended Carmel schools. As a parent, I became more involved in my children's sports through Dads' Club. We attended baseball, softball, and football games. My son played baseball from first grade and through high school. He began playing on the travel teams through Dads' Club in 1991 and the Pups football teams. He continued playing on travel baseball and the varsity team during high school. This experience helped him earn a scholarship to play baseball in college.

Carmel sports became a major part of our lives just as they have for many of you. We spent our summers at Wodock Field, Badger Park and Cherry Tree Complex. We rooted for sons and daughters whether our children were playing or not. Walking tacos were the norm for many meals during those summers! Lots of fond memories include Carmel Dads' Club.

My son, Tony Schmid, catching and my husband, Bob Otten, umpiring during a baseball game in 1991.

I was "team mother" countless years for CDC and various school teams. It could get quite warm working in the concession stands on summer evenings but we all took our turns. My husband umpired baseball and refereed football for CDC for many years as well as for IHSAA until he passed away in 2004.

By the time my children were students at the high school, they were involved in the sports programs or the music department. My daughter was a member of the Marching Greyhounds. As a Band Boosters member I witnessed the countless hours and dedication of the staff, students, and parents to create the nationally ranked band it is today. The Marching Greyhounds performed in the Rose Bowl Parade as well as in the Macy's Thanksgiving Parade. This band is nationally ranked, winning the 2012 Bands of America Grand National Championship. Another performing arts group, The Carmel High School Ambassadors, spent spring break of 2014 performing in Europe. These two groups are examples of opportunities for the students at Carmel High School.

As a parent, I could not have asked for a more educational, yet challenging high school experience for my children. It was rewarding to watch my children succeed in the school system I attended as well as children of many Carmel alumni who remained and raised their families here. As an educator, it has been as honor to be a part of such an excellent school system. Many schools in the district, including Carmel High

School have earned Blue Ribbon Awards for excellence. Carmel Clay Schools are ranked high on Indiana's ISTEP testing. Carmel High School is well represented by National Merit Scholars annually.

I had parents of students tell me they moved here because of the education they knew their children would receive in Carmel while other parents were more focused on the sports programs. Teachers, coaches, and other staff members of Carmel schools are preparing students for the next level of education that is necessary in today's society. Carmel High School is well known for its many accolades in all areas of academia as well as the fine arts and sports programs.

What I find ironic is why my parents brought my sister and me to Carmel nearly sixty years ago. The one common thread that was mentioned many times when Dan and I talked with people while gathering information for this book was "Carmel was different then." It was a small town but our parents brought all of us here because they wanted to be a part of this town. They knew Carmel was on the cusp of being someplace special. Little did I know how that long, hot ride in the backseat of our car in 1957 would impact my life. Today, Carmel is that someplace special.

I came to realize that all the pieces of the puzzle came together for Carmel because a group of men sat around a kitchen table in 1958 with a vision for their own children. Mothers and fathers came together from different places and all walks of life wanting the best educational and athletic opportunities for their children. Did they realize what impact "their vision" would have on the little town of Carmel in the 1950's? That vision has allowed me to fulfill the vision I had for my own children as well as my students and for generations to come. I am eternally grateful to that group of men who met at Mr. Hubley's house who helped take Carmel from that small town to the internationally recognized city that it has become.

Dan, Mike Howard, and I had the privilege of sitting in Dick Nyers's family room and listen to the stories of the "old days." To hear him discuss those days with Dan and Mike was one of the most incredible experiences. They still called him "Coach." I still called him Mr. Nyers. But it was the rapport he had with these two "boys" that was so poignant to watch. Thank you, Mr. Nyers for making me feel fifteen again on that October night in 2013.

On June 12, 2014, Coach Dick Nyers was inducted into the Indiana Football Hall of Fame. For all of his athleticism, his positive attitude, work ethic, and impact on his players, Dick Nyers is the epitome of what a coach should be.

We would like to thank Howard Wodock, Jerry York, and Neil Schmeltekopf for making the vision a reality through the Carmel Dads' Club. You are all iconic figures in the annals of sports history. Thank you to the Hubleys, the Howards, the Grahams, the Irvins, and many others too numerous to mention.

Our time with Anne Porteous was very special. Truly an amazing woman who was at the forefront of many establishments that helped to shape Carmel in many ways. She is the founder of the Friends of the Carmel Library. In the early 1960's, Anne brought the Indianapolis Symphony to hold a concert at the Carmel High School gymnasium. From being a Charter Member of Orchard Park Presbyterian Church, to being a science teacher at Carmel Junior High, Anne helped shaped the lives of many students. Because of Anne and the Better Schools Party, Carmel Clay Schools established its first School Board in 1957. Dan and I were completely in awe of her. Thank you, Anne, for sharing your stories with us.

This picture was taken January 21, 2014. Dan and I had such pleasant visits with Anne Porteous. She had so many stories and memories.

In the words of Dan Chapman, "These collective people whose uncommon desire to help their kids began a legacy which grew into a city of achievers, a city of champions that culminated into the number one city in America in 2012 by *Money Magazine*."

If you have stories or memories to share about growing up in Carmel, or would like to share how you have benefitted from growing up here or from Carmel's excellence whether it was in sports, academics, or fine arts, etc, please feel free to send your stories and pictures to the Carmel Clay Historical Society's website's link:

http://www.carmelclayhistory.org/local-history/submit-to-the-carmel-dads-club-online-collection.

Thank you for sharing your stories and pictures. We will be happy to collect and publish a second edition of this information in the future. Proceeds from this book will be donated to Carmel Dads' Club and to the Carmel Clay Historical Society.

EPILOGUE

Having just completed six months training in the U.S. Army Reserves and two years playing for the Baltimore Colts, I was very fortunate, in 1958, to be hired by the Carmel School Board as the high school football coach. Eventually, I was responsible for developing and leading the entire football program, grades four through twelve.

Reflecting upon this period, I can identify two major events that influenced the program development. The first, which occurred during my tenure, was the formation of the Carmel Dads' Club with their many great volunteers. The second was the decision by the School Board to have only one high school. This took place after my departure.

Both of these events allowed Carmel to develop a highly successful football program. I am very proud to have played a part in the development of the Dads'

Club, and I am reminded of a statement that hangs above the practice fields at the U.S. Military Academy,

"On these fields are sown the seeds that future champions grow."

The Carmel athletic seeds were sown during those early years, and they continue to grow into a bountiful harvest year after year. Not only in football, but in all sports, Carmel is truly the town of Champions! I am happy to have played a very small part in the cultivation of those early seeds.

Dick Nyers, 2013

Dick and Nancy

Acknowledgements

We are very grateful for all the support, patience, knowledge, and personal accounts of events the following people contributed to this book. Many of the following women and men were a significant part of the establishment of the Carmel Dads' Club. Many thanks to:

Jack Berry	Mr. and Mrs. Dick Nyers
Norm Bristley	John Osler
Pete Davis	Paul Osler
Mike Easterday	Mrs. Anne Porteous
Greg Fearrin	Mrs. Phyllis Rockhill
Jim Garretson	Jim Pursel
Mrs. Irma Graham	Steve Schmeltekopf
David Heighway	Bill and the late Edie Shepherd
Mike Howard	Billy Shepherd
Mr. & Mrs. Don Huffer	Larry and Robert Smith
Bruce Hubley	Steve Sturtz
Jim Inskeep	Fred Swift
Bob Irvin	The late John Wilson
Mrs. Toots Irvin	Mrs. Dottie Wodock
Kathy Marshall	Jack Wodock
Bob McDonough	Bruce Wolf
Tom Meeks	Mrs. Peggy York
	Noby York

Index

The following people are shown in pictures on pages listed:

Wilson, Steve   74, 101

Winkler, Carl   50, 74, 76

Wodock, Dorothy   27

Wodock, Howard   16, 18

Wodock, Jim   18, 74, 76

Wood, Mike   50,

Woods, Doug   18

Wright, Bob   74, 76, 93

Yde, Bill   93, 101

York, Jerry   74, 76, 77

York, Noby   77

York, Steve   18, 50, 89

Yost, Geary   18, 26

Zwisler, John 50